A FIRST *PetCare* BOOK

SAM'S Rabbit

HODDER AND STOUGHTON
LONDON SYDNEY AUCKLAND TORONTO

The author and publishers are grateful to the
RSPCA, and in particular to Miss Cindy Milburn,
for much helpful advice during the preparation of
this book.

British Library Cataloguing in Publication Data

Snell, Nigel
  Sam's rabbit.
  1. Pets : Rabbits. Care – For children
  I. Title   II. Series
  636'.9322

  ISBN 0-340-42527-X

Text and illustrations copyright © Nigel Snell 1988

First published 1988

Published by Hodder and Stoughton Children's Books,
a division of Hodder and Stoughton Ltd,
Mill Road, Dunton Green, Sevenoaks, Kent TN13 2YJ

Printed in Belgium by Henri Proost et Cie, Turnhout

Note to parents and teachers

Books in the First Pet Care series have been written for young children as an introduction to responsible pet ownership. It is hoped that they will encourage children to become involved in the care of their pets, and to take an interest in animals generally.

It should be noted, however, that the books do not offer detailed advice on animal husbandry. It is unfair both to children and pets if adults attempt to make children take responsibility at too early an age. The ultimate responsibility for the animals' welfare must lie with the parents or teacher. It is up to them to ensure that the child/pet relationship is a happy and rewarding one.

D.B. Wilkins MA, MRCVS,
Chief Veterinary Officer, RSPCA

Baby rabbits

Sam's friend, Jason, has two pet rabbits. Six weeks ago, the female rabbit gave birth to five babies. Jason asks Sam if he would like one to keep as a pet.

5

Sam is very excited. He runs indoors to find Mummy.
'Please may I have a baby rabbit? he asks. 'Jason says I can.'
'Only if you promise to help look after it,' Mummy replies. Sam nods his head.

They decide to collect the rabbit at the weekend, after Daddy has made a hutch for it to live in.

Making a hutch

On Saturday, Daddy and Sam go to the
shops. They buy some wood, wire
netting and nails. Daddy is going to
make a hutch like the one below. The
rabbit will be able to stay in the open
and nibble the grass. Or, if the weather
gets too hot or cold, it can move into the
little bedroom at the end.

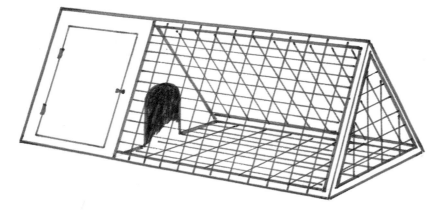

Daddy builds the hutch carefully so that the bedroom is dry and cosy. Rabbits don't like draughts. He makes sure the wire netting is nailed firmly across the cage. The holes in the netting are quite large.

'That looks great, Daddy,' says Sam.

On Sunday, the hutch is finished. Sam and Daddy go next door to choose a rabbit. Sam takes a long time to decide. At last, he chooses the biggest. It has big dark eyes, and beautiful black and white fur. Jason says it is a male rabbit. Sam decides to call him Bugsie.

Bedding

Daddy carries Bugsie back home in a cardboard box. The hutch is on the lawn. There is some hay inside the bedroom for Bugsie to sleep on. The hay must be changed twice a week so that it does not get dirty. Hay can be bought from any good pet shop.

A new home

Mummy ties a water dropper onto the
side of the hutch.
'You must remember to change the
water every day, Sam,' she says.

She puts some food into one of the
feeding bowls inside the hutch.
Bugsie's food must also be changed
every day.

Bugsie explores every corner of his new
home, his nose twitching. He sniffs at
the feeding bowl.
'He seems to like it,' says Sam.

Mummy brings Bugsie some more food.
There are slices of raw carrot, and some
special rabbit pellets from the pet shop.

Rabbits also like all kinds of green vegetables, such as lettuce and cabbage, as well as brown bread and hay. They are fond of wild plants such as dandelions. But plants which are poisonous, or which have been sprayed with weedkiller, can be deadly. Daddy warns Sam not to pick any plants for Bugsie without asking Mummy or Daddy first.

Exercise

Bugsie spends most of his time in the hutch. But once a day, Sam lets him out for a run on the lawn. Daddy has made sure there are no holes in the garden fence. Otherwise, Bugsie might run away.

After about an hour or so, Sam puts Bugsie back in the hutch. He supports the rabbit with one hand and gently holds his ears with the other. This is the correct way to hold a rabbit. Bugsie soon gets used to being in Sam's arms.

Health

Once a month, Sam empties Bugsie's hutch and scrubs it clean. A dirty hutch may make a rabbit ill.

Sam checks that Bugsie's eyes are bright and sparkling. When a rabbit is sick, its eyes become dull or watery. If this happens, the rabbit should be taken to the vet.

Sam also checks that Bugsie's teeth and claws don't get too long. Daddy gives Bugsie a piece of wood to gnaw on, and from time to time he clips Bugsie's nails. He uses special clippers to do this.

Sam brushes Bugsie's fur to make sure it doesn't get matted.

In winter

At the beginning of winter, Sam helps Daddy move the hutch into the garden shed. Rabbits don't mind cold weather, but they hate getting wet! Sam is glad he won't have to clean out the hutch in the rain.

Bugsie will stay in the garden shed until spring.

Bugsie and Sam become good friends. Sam loves stroking Bugsie's long silky ears and his beautiful soft fur. He brings Bugsie an extra piece of raw carrot each time he visits the hutch. Bugsie waits patiently inside, his nose forever twitching.

Index

Further information

The RSPCA produces a range of pet guides for older children and adults which are available through the Society, as are details of the Society's Junior Membership scheme. Interested readers should send a stamped, addressed envelope to:

RSPCA Education Department
The Causeway
Horsham
West Sussex RH12 1HG